Cryptocur

A Primer

By

Eric Morse

To the risk-takers, creators, and innovators... and the people that support and encourage them.

Table of Contents

Introduction

What is Cryptocurrency?

Magic Internet Money? Digital Currency? Cash for the Internet? An Incredible Investment Opportunity?

All of the Above.

The word "cryptocurrency" refers to digital "tokens" used to exchange value over the internet. Rather than being controlled by governments or central banks, the values of these currencies are determined solely by the economics of supply and demand. The production and operation of these digital currencies involves encryption, thus the presence of "crypto" in the name. Fortunately, all of the heavy cryptographic math is hidden from the end user by software, allowing users to send and receive money without knowing what a "private key" is.

The definition above, while accurate, is not complete. It doesn't explain why cryptocurrencies were created, what makes them important, or why people use them when there are easier methods for conducting transactions over the internet. It doesn't say why you should care about cryptocurrency. It doesn't tell you which of the hundreds of cryptocurrencies are worth caring about.

Those questions are what this book is for.

Cryptocurrency: A Primer is an entry-level introduction to the world of cryptocurrency. People who are already active in cryptocurrency probably won't find anything new in these pages. The intended audience is who I call the "crypto-curious"... people who have heard of Bitcoin or cryptocurrency and want to know what all the fuss is about. They don't want technical details. They don't want to feel like they're learning a new language or earning a degree in computer science. They may not want to buy or use a cryptocurrency at this point; they just want to know what it is so they can decide for themselves whether it is worth their time. This book is not a step-by-step tutorial or an investment guide. It is an explanation of concepts, and an exploration of history and significance of some of the more important cryptocurrencies. When you reach the end, you will know why people use Bitcoin. You'll know why people are talking about Ethereum. You'll know the story behind DarkCoin. In other words: you'll know what all the fuss is about. Then you can go on to more detailed books on using or investing.

What technical knowledge do you need to bring with you on this trip? Not much. A certain amount of jargon is unavoidable when discussing cryptocurrency, but I try to keep it to a minimum and define new terms where appropriate. It would be helpful if you've at least heard the words "Bitcoin" and "cryptocurrency" before now, and it would be very helpful if you've bought something online at some point in your life. Assuming you paid for this book and read this far into the introduction, you should be okay.

So let's get started!

Chapter 1: Bitcoin (BTC)

Bitcoin is the genesis of all cryptocurrencies and, therefore, has to be the starting point on our journey. In talking about Bitcoin we're going to be discussing concepts which are integral to most, if not all the other major currencies.

Bitcoin is a relatively recent invention born of necessity. Prior to Bitcoin, the primary way of exchanging currency with people over the internet was through trusted third parties such as PayPal, banks, or credit card providers like Visa and MasterCard. In the physical world, the easiest kind of money transfer is to simply hand someone cash; there is no need for a third party. This differs from a bank transfer where you're trusting one or more parties to handle the transaction for you according to terms and conditions agreed upon by... but rarely actually understood by... the account holders.

Bitcoin takes these trusted third parties out of the equation. In 2009, a white paper appeared proposing a brand new currency called Bitcoin based on a new technology known as a "blockchain." The blockchain is essentially a decentralized, public running ledger of all Bitcoin transactions. It replaces the third party in money transfers by authenticating and recording transactions for all to see. The blockchain isn't a bank. It isn't a government or a corporation. It isn't a person, an organization; or single website or server that can be seized or shut down. It is simply a ledger maintained by a network of computers that is distributed across the globe.

Take a moment to think about what this means. The lack of 3rd parties means Bitcoin operates over the internet in a manner similar to cash. Payment processors cannot block your transactions because there are no payment processors. Banks or governments cannot freeze your accounts because you are your own bank.

It's also important that you recognize the utility of the blockchain as a means of recording and verifying information. This information can be anything; it is not limited to account balances and money transfers. Data stored on the blockchain could represent user accounts, deeds to property like houses or cars, marriages, copyrights, licenses... anything. In the specific case of Bitcoin, though, the blockchain is used as a ledger of all money transfers on the Bitcoin network. How one can be certain that the ledger is accurate and reliable? This is where the concept of consensus comes into play. Consensus is the idea of multiple computers verifying the ledger and agreeing which version is the most accurate.

In cryptocurrency, a blockchain is exactly what the name implies: a chain of blocks, each of which contain data. Blocks are connected or "stacked" chronologically.. In the specific example of Bitcoin, a single block is composed of many transaction records. When a block is completed and verified by the network, it will be added permanently to the chain. After that, the contents of the block cannot be changed without the majority of the networked computers agreeing to the changes.

Maintaining the blockchain is the job of special nodes on the Bitcoin network, called "miners". Each miner or group (pool) of miners is constantly working on a specific mathematical problem. Not only is this problem difficult, it actually becomes MORE difficult as more people try to solve it. The first to solve the problem correctly gets to write the next block of transactions to the blockchain. In return for their effort, they earn some newly created bitcoin, plus they get to keep all the transaction fees in the block they just wrote. The miner that writes the block gets to pick which transactions get written... and it's in their best interest to pick the transactions that have transaction fees associated with them. Thus, while the transaction fees are technically optional, if you want the miners to care enough about your transaction to confirm it, you should always include the appropriate fee. Most other cryptocurrencies operate similarly, with differences in the exact math problem being solved, how the difficulty scales, how miners are rewarded, etc.

Bitcoin also pioneered the idea of digital wallets, which hold the currency in separate addresses. These addresses are loosely equivalent to banking account numbers. Although this is a vast oversimplification, it is accurate enough for most people to use Bitcoin without detailed knowledge of what is happening behind the scenes in their wallet.

Bitcoin has been a massive success. Since its creation in 2009, its value has skyrocketed from less than $1 to more than $4000 in 2017. It is increasingly accepted as a form of payment by businesses and financial institutions around the world, and some investors see it now as a store of value, much as gold or silver is. But there have been some challenges. Bitcoin - and cryptocurrency in general - is in a gray area legally, Some countries have outlawed it entirely, while others have sharply restricted its use or access to it. The common misconception that Bitcoin is anonymous had led to its adoption by hackers and criminals as a payment method for illicit goods and services. Several major Bitcoin exchanges have been shut down or have gone out of business because of fraud, hacking, or other problems.

Despite these setbacks, Bitcoin and cryptocurrencies in general have grown in popularity. Many users find the decentralized nature of these digital assets very appealing as for the most part they are free from the laws and regulations applied to traditional currencies and financial instruments. But even though Bitcoin is the first and most popular cryptocurrency, it is not necessarily the best. There are many more that have use Bitcoin as a starting point and innovated beyond it. The purpose of this book is to discuss some of these major success stories.

Despite all these newcomers, Bitcoin is still lauded for its history, its consistency, and its trustworthiness. Moreover, it's hard to beat Bitcoin's massive market share; It retains its domination of the cryptocurrency markets.

Bitcoin's official website is **bitcoin.org**.

Chapter 2: Litecoin (LTC)

The Bitcoin software is open-source. This means that anyone can not only view the source code, but can copy it and make changes to their copy in order to create something brand new. That is exactly how many of the alternative cryptocurrencies, or "altcoins", that are discussed in this book came into being. Litecoin is the first and, at one time, the most popular of these Bitcoin derivatives.

Litecoin takes many of the aspects of Bitcoin but builds upon them. It was first released by Charles Lee, brother to Bobby Lee, the head of BTC China, one of the largest Bitcoin/Litecoin exchanges in China. His intent was to create an improved alternative to Bitcoin. The result was a digital currency some say is the silver to Bitcoin's gold.

Litecoin offered several improvements to the Bitcoin architecture. One major change was the hashing algorithm that was used for verification of transactions on the blockchain. Recall from the previous chapter that writing blocks of transactions to the blockchain is done by special nodes called "miners". These miners are all competing with one another to solve a complex mathematical problem, with a reward going to the first miner (or group of miners) to solve it. In Bitcoin, the math being performed is based on an encryption algorithm called SHA-256. There is no need for end users to know anything about SHA-256, but we need to delve a little deeper than the average user in order to understand why Litecoin exists.

SHA-256 had one big limitation in terms of accessibility and decentralization: it was very easy to dedicate hardware to Bitcoin mining. Shortly after Bitcoin became popular, dedicated Bitcoin mining units… special machines that did nothing but perform SHA-256 calculations… began to appear. These dedicated miners were much more efficient than home computers, even powerful ones, at Bitcoin mining. Soon installations of large numbers of these miners began to concentrate management of the Bitcoin network into a small number of full-time operations, whose sole purpose is the verification of Bitcoin blocks in order to reap the rewards. Recall from the Bitcoin chapter that one of the main features of Bitcoin is its decentralization. Some saw the concentration of mining as a threat so serious that it was worth creating a competing currency to avoid it.

Litecoin tries to prevent this situation by using a different hashing algorithm. This algorithm, called Scrypt, is dependent upon the device's memory and not processor speed. This reduces the necessity to set up massive mining farms and makes mining blocks a more tenable action for the average user.

Litecoin also offered a far faster rate of transaction verification. Where Bitcoin's algorithms solve a block an average of 10 minutes, Litecoin's Scrypt algorithm solves a block every two and a half minutes. This means that transactions are processed much faster than they would be otherwise. In order to make up for this faster block parsing, the Litecoin network produces four times as many currency units as Bitcoin does per block.

Litecoin is interesting in that it has pretty much succeeded flawlessly in its primary goal of being more efficient than Bitcoin. It currently sits in the top five in terms of market capitalization, not far behind Bitcoin and Ethereum. This is perhaps the perfect reflection of what Litecoin set out to achieve. It wasn't aiming to upset the market, but rather to serve as a better version of the major currency. Litecoin didn't innovate on the nature of cryptocurrency, but it did improve on how that nature was implemented. Litecoin is essentially a clone of Bitcoin with different... and arguably better... parameters. Regardless, it sits comfortably with its market cap as the best alternative to Bitcoin for simple money transfers. Litecoin prices have surged from $4 to $80 in the last year.

Litecoin's website is **litecoin.com**.

Chapter 3: Ethereum (ETH, ETC)

Ethereum is another major form of cryptocurrency. Even though it is one of the most recent, having only been released in 2015, it has become one of the most popular, with the second highest market capitalization after Bitcoin.

Ethereum was first described in 2013 in a technical paper by Vitalik Buterin, a young programmer who played a major part in Bitcoin's early development. His paper proposed that Bitcoin's blockchain needed the capability to allow applications to run on the blockchain. His paper and arguments weren't terribly popular at the time, but they were enough for him to join with several other eager programmers in 2014 to develop a scripting language that gave more freedom and utility to a blockchain.

So, what precisely makes Ethereum different from Bitcoin? The biggest innovation is the implementation of "smart contracts," which provide a way to automate certain agreements or arrangements between two or more parties. They allow the secure and reliable exchange of pretty much anything with a value when certain criteria are met. These criteria are defined by the entities that create the contract. A smart contract is essentially a transaction with intelligence behind it. It is Bitcoin with a brain.

These smart contracts are permanently stored in the blockchain where they cannot be altered without the consent of all the parties involved. This ensures the contract hasn't been tampered with or the terms changed. In addition, the relatively straightforward nature of smart contracts and their implementation eliminates the necessity of a third party or middleman, such as a lawyer or a broker, to guarantee the terms are carried out in full as written in the contract. The smart contract embedded in the blockchain serves as the guarantee. If Bitcoin made payment processors irrelevant, Ethereum did the same for contract lawyers.

Smart contracts run within the Ethereum Virtual Machine, a kind of computer built into the Ethereum blockchain. Each Ethereum node on the network runs the Ethereum Virtual Machine in tandem, providing both security and redundancy. These scripts and smart contracts are typically written in languages like Solidity, Serpent, LLL, or Mutan, all of which specifically geared for the writing of smart contracts. Solidity is the most common and is the primary language utilized by Ethereum; programmers with experience in C and JavaScript will find Solidity to be rather familiar. This offers unparalleled interactivity and potential, which Bitcoin and Litecoin cannot provide, because their code only addresses money transfer and storage.

In two short years, Ethereum has enabled (and inspired) the development of many other blockchain-based projects and has attracted the attention of many traditional financial services institutions. This success hasn't, of course, come without some difficulties. One was large enough to create an alternative Ethereum ecosystem, which gives us a chance to talk about an important concept in cryptocurrency... forking. This is when a digital asset splits into two different, largely incompatible forms.

One of the first major projects built on the Ethereum network was a venture capital fund referred to as "The DAO." The acronym itself means decentralized autonomous organization, which is essentially a heavily decentralized company running on a blockchain. There can be many DAOs, but in this case we are referring to a specific decentralized autonomous organization, which simply called itself The DAO. If this sounds like science fiction… keep reading; we haven't even gotten to the part about time travel and alternate realities yet.

The DAO comprised the largest bundle of smart contracts to be running on Ethereum and was the earliest, most publicized project on the platform. Its purpose was to collect money from investors and distribute it to projects that the investors voted on… similar to a venture capital firm. The DAO's operation was contained entirely on the Ethereum blockchain. It did not have an address. It didn't have a Board of Directors. It was not incorporated under the laws of any nation or government. It was just a set of rules codified in contracts stored in the blockchain. The DAO was so large, in fact, that it was able to raise roughly 170 million dollars in Ethereum tokens (called Ether or ETH) from investors.

Unfortunately, there were serious security flaws in The DAO's smart contracts, which enabled hackers to steal 3.6 million ETH–roughly $50 million at the time–and move it to different accounts. So much had been invested and stolen that the Ethereum community was vehement about action being taken. There were contentious debates about two options: a soft fork, wherein the pilfered currency would be "burned" or made unusable by either the thieves or the original owners, and a hard fork or a total rollback of the blockchain to a point before the exploit occurred, resulting in a kind of alternate timeline.

A soft fork would maintain the original blockchain in its original form, complete with The DAO's creation and the multi-million-dollar exploit. A hard fork would go back in time and create a new reality where the DAO exploit never happened.

Vitalik and the other Ethereum developers favored a hard fork which was the action eventually taken. However, many Ethereum users disagreed with this decision, as they believed in the concept of the blockchain being immutable and permanent. As a result, they created a version of Ethereum on the unaltered blockchain, which they called Ethereum Classic (ETC). Although the two versions of Ethereum share a common beginning, there are incompatible with each other, rather like humans and chimpanzees have a common ancestor but are entirely different species.

Ethereum Classic is still a major cryptocurrency and, while it lags behind Bitcoin, Ethereum and Litecoin in value, it is still in the top 10 in terms of market capitalization (as of the time of writing), and is also worth your attention.

Despite this early drama, Ethereum remains one of the most technologically innovative forms of cryptocurrency and shows no signs of slowing down. Some day, a cryptocurrency may overtake Bitcoin and Ethereum just might be the one to do it.

Find out more about Ethereum at **ethereum.org**

Chapter 4: Ripple (XRP)

Ripple is the point of much contention; people either love it or hate it. Ripple is also one of the most poorly understood cryptocurrencies, because it differs in many ways from standard cryptocurrencies like Bitcoin, Litecoin, and Ethereum. Therefore, it's important that we examine the history and intent of Ripple.

Ripple refers to two related concepts: the money-transfer platform called Ripple, and the cryptocurrency, XRP, that used on the platform. The platform Ripple uses XRP as a means of carrying out some of its core functions. Unlike Bitcoin, Litecoin and Ethereum tokens, which are mined over time, Ripple XRP tokens were "pre-mined," meaning that 100 billion were created at the start, and over time will gradually be destroyed or "burned" during transactions.

Ripple has been in development longer than Bitcoin. In 2004 a programmer, Ryan Fugger, developed RipplePay. His idea was to create a decentralized system which would allow new forms of money to be created, functioning through IOUs traded among trusted users. Essentially, RipplePay would keep a log of running value debts, which would "ripple" throughout the network. Somewhat later, the development of Bitcoin in 2009 inspired Arthur Britto and David Schwartz to create a system which would verify the current ledger of transactions not mining, as with Bitcoin, but rather by consensus among users. In 2011 Britto, Schwartz, Jed McCaleb of eDonkey fame, and Fugger formed OpenCoin, which became Ripple Labs two years later.

The intent was to create a system for frictionless money transfers, meaning that transfers would be low cost and nearly instantaneous. Bitcoin had a prohibitively long verification process for point-of-sale transactions, due to the reliance on mining to verify transactions. Verification could sometimes take as long as an hour if the Bitcoin network was especially busy. Mining is also a very power-intensive operation, as the processors use a lot of electricity. Ripple, by contrast, eliminates the need for mining, saving energy and speeding up verification times. Replacing resource-intensive mining with network-wide consensus also reduces the possibility of centralization, which had become a major concern in the implementation of Bitcoin.

This may seem antithetical at first to the concept of cryptocurrency, given that one of the original purposes of Bitcoin was to remove any trust or third party from the equation and allow a simple way for money to be exchanged, but it's actually quite compatible. We'll get to that in just a moment.

OpenCoin (later renamed Ripple Labs) developed the Ripple Transaction Protocol to allow the instantaneous and unobstructed transfer of anything of value, whether it be dollars, euros, yen, or even airline miles, between two parties, and to allow quick and easy currency exchanges across national borders. For currencies with no direct exchange route, XRP would be used as an intermediate currency. The developers then created the Bitcoin Bridge, now one of Ripple's key features. The bridge allowed Ripple users to send any form of currency to a given Bitcoin address; conversion into Bitcoin would happen "on the fly."

Ripple has become one of the top 10 cryptocurrencies, with an $8.36 billion market capitalization at this writing, and has entered into partnerships with an impressive number of banks and other financial institutions.

You can easily see Ripple's appeal. It makes money transfers much cheaper and quicker than existing systems. Prior to Ripple, individuals needing to send money across borders had to use cumbersome third-party services like Western Union or PayPal, or arrange expensive wire transfers through their banks. All of these services charge fees, which can be prohibitive for some users, and in the case of bank wires, the transfer might take days to clear before being deposited in the recipient's bank account. For their part, banks also suffered from slow interbank transfers through existing centralized systems, such as SWIFT.

Ripple replaces these older systems with a peer-to-peer settlement system that was entirely user-focused and that used consensus in order to verify transactions, which would allow an extremely rapid transfer rate. Moreover, Ripple transfers have no built-in restraints, allowing for any currency (or other item of value) to be transferred and exchanged for other any other currency (or item of value) for pennies on the dollar.

So, how does XRP fit into this worldwide money transmittal service?

Unlike Litecoin or Ethereum, for example, the XRP token wasn't intended to compete against or improve upon Bitcoin. In fact, the two complement one another, as the Ripple protocol allows the easy exchange of any form of currency including Bitcoin. Instead, XRP was developed as a compliment to the Ripple protocol, and as a means by which the parent company could generate capital. Half of the total supply of XRP is retained by Ripple Labs and will never be in circulation. [Note: At this writing, 1 XRP = $0.21, so the XRP held represents more than $900 million.]

While holders of XRP have to maintain a minimum balance of 30 XRP in their wallets in order to use the system, XRP in most cases is not even necessary for the Ripple platform to operate. The Ripple network relies on trusted gateways for transfers. If two gateways can use euros for cross-border transactions, for example, they don't have to send XRP to make the transfer. XRP is used only for the very low transfer fees. In this sense, Ripple is quite different from Bitcoin, Litecoin or Ethereum.

Ripple may be the first major cryptocurrency to make an impact on the global scale with banking, but it's not the only one. We'll talk a bit later on about NXT's Mijin blockchain and how it has the potential to change banking's internal infrastructure, as Ripple has begun to change banking's external infrastructure with fast, cross-border transactions.

You can find Ripple's official website at **ripple.com**.

Chapter 5: Storj (STORJ, SJCX)

Most cryptocurrencies exist for a specific reason. Bitcoin was intended (among other things) to eliminate the reliance on 3rd parties for monetary transactions. Litecoin was meant to be a faster, more centralization-resistant version of Bitcoin. Ethereum was a smarter Bitcoin. Storj is unique in that its purpose is extremely specific AND totally unrelated to monetary transactions. Like Ripple, it is not a clone of Bitcoin, but is something totally new.

Storj aims to take a really fundamental and common idea and turn it on its head. Storj, in the company's own words, is a "platform, cryptocurrency, and suite of decentralized applications that allows you to store data in a secure and decentralized manner." In other words, Storj takes something that is already decentralized... cloud computing... and takes it several steps further. Instead of having data stored on a central server, as with Google Drive or Dropbox, it is instead stored on a peer-to-peer network of computers. Files are first encrypted so that no one but the end user of the files can access or open the data. Since the data is decentralized and distributed across the network, losing access to one's files is highly unlikely as you are not depending on a single point of storage. In other words, Storj is to cloud storage companies what Bitcoin is to payment processors and banks.

But where does all of this storage capacity come from, and what does any of this have to do with cryptocurrency?

Anyone can participate in the Storj network by sharing part of their unused hard drive space in exchange for money. Originally these participants were paid in SJCX, a Counterparty-based cryptocurrency. Counterparty will be discussed in a later chapter. Payments for using the network to store files were also made in SJCX, and sales of the SJCX altcoin were used to raise money for the project. Recently, Storj transitioned from SJCX to an Ethereum-based altcoin called STORJ. Payments are currently accepted in US Dollars and BTC.

The STORJ project isn't particularly interested in competing with Bitcoin or Ethereum. After all, neither Bitcoin nor Ethereum offer cloud storage. The project's developers introduced their own token so that they could use it for their own personal reasons, as well as to give the company a financial kickstart from sales of the tokens. (This kind of Initial Coin Offering, also called an "ICO", has become a very popular crowdfunding vehicle.) Moreover, the developers wanted to ensure the platform's flexibility and stability with a custom-made currency, instead of relying on an external currency over which they had no control.

In that sense, STORJ isn't a particularly fascinating investment. Storj as a service is likely to grow gradually, at least in the short term, so you probably will not see rapid exponential growth as happened with Bitcoin and Ethereum. Rather, the value of STORJ tokens will rise slowly over time, as the service gains market share. Storj is important for several reasons. First, Storj is a project and business built on cryptocurrency who's purpose is largely unrelated to currency or monetary transactions. It is an evolution of purpose; it represents the next layer of development... the use of cryptocurrency technology as a platform rather than as a product in and of itself. Storj also represents a return to early days of Bitcoin when the average user could participate meaningfully in the network and be profitably reimbursed for their efforts. Bitcoin mining has been far out of the reach of the average user for some time, and even most altcoins require better-than-average computers in order to keep up. With Storj, however, a spare hard drive is all one needs to help the network and earn money doing so.

Learn more about Storj at **storj.io**.

Chapter 6: DarkCoin/DASH (DASH)

One cryptocurrency about which there is a large amount of contention is Dash, which has one of the highest market caps of any digital asset. Dash started out as just another cryptocurrency in a time where the Internet was being flooded with Bitcoin clones. However, Dash set out to be a little bit better than the competition.

The key problem that Dash was attempting to solve was lack of anonymity in transactions. Bitcoin proponents have often claimed that Bitcoin is anonymous, but it isn't. Bitcoin is pseudonymous. When Bitcoin transfers are made, they are stored in the blockchain as a record of which party made a transaction to whom, at what time and of how much. The parties involved are identified by their Bitcoin addresses, not by names, social security numbers, or any other personally identifiable information. The Bitcoin addresses are pseudonyms, in that sense. Since the entire blockchain is a public record, it is possible to deduce who owns those Bitcoin addresses by following chains of transactions until you reach one where one of the parties reveals their identity, either intentionally or accidentally. With sufficient effort, names can be attached to addresses, and the illusion of anonymity disappears.

In other words, Bitcoin transactions are not inherently anonymous and can be traced back to the end user. However, it is possible to further hide the real-world identities of Bitcoin users by "mixing" Bitcoin transactions, so that the association between address and user is obscured. The best analogy for mixing is this: Let's say that you've got a dryer with a bunch of identical shirts tumbling around in it. You can put a shirt in and take a different shirt out. You won't know whose shirt you have pulled out, and nobody is going to know if they pulled yours out. Since your shirt has just been tumbling around with a bunch of other shirts, there's no way to prove that any given shirt is yours.

While there were (and still are) mixing services available for Bitcoin users, mixing is not an inherent feature of the Bitcoin platform. Dash changed that. Mixing is built into the Dash client and is intended to provide security and anonymity in all transactions. Used in conjunction with a proxy service or the TOR network, it would be possible for Dash transactions to be completely untraceable.

Despite the obvious advantages Dash offers, many critics are apprehensive about Dash and some even go so far as to call it a scam. To understand why, you have to understand its history.

Dash was first released in the very beginning of 2014 under the name XCoin. It was released two days earlier than advertised, during which 1.9 million coins were pre-mined, or brought into existence outside of the mining process that creates new bitcoin and Bitcoin-like currencies like Litecoin. This is one big point of contention that leads some people to believe Dash is a scam.

Mining ahead of a project launch and starting out with a set number of coins is known in the cryptocurrency community as an "insta-mine." This insta-mine, in particular, was purportedly accidental, but insta-mines are heavily frowned upon because a small number of people could end up with a majority of coins before the public has a chance to buy them. Hypothetically, these early holders could manipulate the value of the coins and profit unfairly from trading the coins on the open market. In the stock market world, this would be known as insider trading, which is illegal. This kind of pre-mining is what soured some cryptocurrency purists on Ripple/XRP, which launched with all the available tokens already available, and significant amount in the hands of the developers.

The cryptocurrency community is split on whether the XCoin insta-mine was truly an accident. The story given by the lead developer, Evan Duffield, is that it was the result of a bug in the source code. Looking at the history of the source code, one can see where Duffield tried multiple times to make changes to the code in order to save the currency and stop the insta-mine. It took several tries before he was successful, and by that time, nearly ten percent of Dash's estimated maximum coin count had been mined.

Duffield attempted to salvage the situation by offering to relaunch the coin. The XCoin community, however, vehemently disagreed with this idea and it was abandoned. Duffield then suggested the possibility of giving coins away in order to broaden the distribution of the coin. Yet again, the community disagreed. At this point, it was decided: XCoin would be left alone to develop as it would.

A month after the launch, XCoin was renamed as DarkCoin. And in 2015, it was renamed yet again as Dash, an abbreviation of "Digital Cash."

Is Dash is better than Bitcoin? Each currency has its advantages. Bitcoin certainly has a larger market share and acceptance as it benefits from being the first cryptocurrency. But Dash comes loaded with many features that aren't present in Bitcoin, such as instant transactions and the aforementioned anonymity capabilities.

The truth is that Dash was gunning hard to become the "Bitcoin" of the future, but its shaky start may have doomed it to contentious obscurity. To counteract the bad publicity, the Dash team has made special public relations efforts to promote the currency, and improved the Dash wallet's user interface to make it easier to use. Dash has a market cap as of this writing of $2.4 billion, but it has lost momentum and is no longer in the top 10. With almost half of the cryptocurrency community being distrustful of it, it's not in a good position to be used by online vendors where other cryptocurrencies, such as Bitcoin, Litecoin or Ethereum, are used more freely. This attitude may change, however, with the Dash team's PR campaigns.

Dash's official website is **dash.org**.

Chapter 7: NXT

NXT is one of the most groundbreaking cryptocurrencies available. NXT was first proposed as a "second generation cryptocurrency" by an anonymous coder in 2013. Unlike many other popular cryptocurrencies, NXT was not built upon the codebase provided by Bitcoin or Ethereum, but rather was built from the ground up using Java. As such, it was able to diverge in some ways from other cryptocurrencies while retaining some similarities.

The central idea was for NXT to take core ideas and concepts from Bitcoin and Ethereum and build upon them, offering a full-fledged blockchain platform that can be used to do almost anything. One major difference between NXT and Bitcoin is the token supply. Bitcoins are constantly being created through proof-of-work (mining). In the NXT ecosystem, however, there is a static supply of money, which means that new coins aren't created by mining. Rather, transactions are verified through proof of stake, or one's ownership of NXT tokens. In fact, NXT can be seen as a proof of concept for the "proof of stake" idea, as 100% proof-of-stake blockchains were previously thought to be unworkable.

Relying on proof-of-stake also means that anyone can verify a block using any device, even something as simple as a Raspberry Pi or a smartphone. There is no such thing as specialized "NXT mining" hardware, and even small players still have a chance to verify a block and receive a reward.

Proof of stake is also innately more efficient than proof of work consensus algorithms, meaning that transactions will happen faster than they would with Bitcoin or even Litecoin.

Another key idea was to create a platform that could implement many important different blockchain features within one blockchain. Because of this, NXT isn't just a cryptocurrency for money transfers; it also offers a suite of services, including additional currencies, an asset exchange for share trading, data storage, a messaging system, an alias registration system, and even a voting module useful for any context, be it political or business. It also has a wide array of support for different plugins, which allows users to easily add their own features to the NXT client and create new applications.

Perhaps the most impressive thing that the NXT system is its support for new monetary systems. The currencies created are backed by the NXT coin itself, but are independent of it. The anonymous founder of NXT, BCNext, said that it was best not to consider the cryptocurrency, NXT, as the most important currency of the system, but rather as the foundation for brand new currencies.

Basically, NXT coin and Bitcoin serve different purposes. NXT coin isn't supposed to be a major feature in and of itself, but rather serve as part of an even bigger platform. Meanwhile, the Bitcoin blockchain was invented primarily for the purpose of establishing a workable digital currency. Meanwhile, the NXT and Ethereum platforms both allow for the creation of new currencies and services on top of their blockchains.

When all is said and done, NXT's intent was to create a next-generation cryptocurrency. In that respect, it has succeeded and NXT is now in the top 20 cryptocurrencies by market capitalization. While NXT is not as famous or as widely used as Bitcoin and Ethereum, it is an innovative cryptocurrency worth keeping an eye on.

Learn more about NXT at **nxtplatform.org**.

Chapter 8: Other Cryptocurrencies of Note

As of this writing there are over 800 distinct cryptocurrencies, with new Initial Coin Offerings appearing almost weekly. It may be impossible for any compendium of cryptocurrencies to be all-inclusive, but there are certainly those deserving at least a mention even if they do not rate a full chapter. This chapter lists other cryptocurrencies worthy of mention either due to historical significance, ambition, innovation, or just plain quirkiness.

ZCash (ZEC)

Zcash is yet another cryptocurrency with a major focus on anonymity. Similar to Bitcoin, it has a fixed maximum of twenty-one million coins, but its mining algorithm was designed to give home-based miners with ordinary computers a chance to mine, making the process more democratic and decentralized than Bitcoin mining. In this sense, it is a combination of Dash and Litecoin.

Zcash was introduced by Zooko Wilcox-Ohearn in September 2016, with the intent of building upon the work of cryptography researchers from multiple universities, especially Johns Hopkins. The researchers had been working on a privacy protocol known as Zerocoin since 2014. Zcash was the logical outcome of that research.

The specific ways in which Zcash implements privacy are rather robust and a bit difficult to explain. Basically, Zcash utilizes zero-knowledge proofs in order to disguise the identity of the sender and the recipient, as well as the overall amount of the transaction. Explaining zero-knowledge proofs is beyond the scope of this book, but the end result is that anonymity is created by making the sending and receiving address any random address on the blockchain itself, similar to the mixing principle discussed earlier. Zcash, like Dash, also gives the users the option of using publicly viewable addresses, if they desire.

Zcash has in one year become a very important cryptocurrency. It has resided comfortably in the top 20 cryptocurrencies indexed by market capitalization. It fulfills a similar purpose to Monero (discussed later) in offering real anonymity in your private transactions, despite a public blockchain.

Zcash's website is **z.cash**

Dogecoin (DOGE)

For many people, their first and most amusing foray into altcoins was the *Dogecoin*. The Dogecoin (or "DOGE") is based around an Internet meme which superimposes misspelled Comic Sans text over a smiling Shiba Inu dog. While Dogecoin was originally a joke; the initial programmer wanted to create a cryptocurrency that would reach more people than Bitcoin by being fun and lighthearted. Additionally, the development of Dogecoin was an attempt to purify the image of Bitcoin, which had become associated with darknet marketplaces, such as the Silk Road and Alphabay, which sold illegal drugs, pornography and other illegal goods and services.

Dogecoin uses the Scrypt algorithm, as does Litecoin, which makes it difficult to create dedicated mining devices, enabling anyone to mine Doge. Dogecoin has a much shorter block time than Litecoin does, which means blocks are verified faster. Additionally, it offers a different mining block difficulty algorithm from Litecoin's, which is specifically intended to discourage mining pools.

Dogecoin was officially released in December of 2013 and jumped sharply in value in the first 3 days. After this brief popularity surge, the value dropped by 80% after many enthusiasts started to take advantage of the ease of mining the young coin.

Dogecoin is mostly now used as a way to tip people online. But the Dogecoin community and the Dogecoin Foundation have become a major fundraising force. Dogecoin campaigns have sent a bobsled team to the Winter Olympics and have established wells in Kenya in a campaign called Doge4Water.

Dogecoin's official website is **dogecoin.com**. There, you will find what is undoubtedly the catchiest and most memorable intro-videos of any cryptocurrency.

Primecoin (XPM)

Primecoin is particularly interesting because of its proof-of-work system. Instead of spending processing power on a difficult but otherwise meaningless encryption problem, Primecoin miners search for chains of prime numbers. This system results in some key differences between Primecoin and Bitcoin.

The first is that within Primecoin, the amount of the currency at any given time, and thereby the scarcity of said currency, is largely defined by the distribution of different prime chains. Therefore, the coins dispensed aren't held back rigidly by pre-defined algorithms, but rather by the natural distribution of a certain numerical property. Likewise, there is no limit to the amount of coins available as there is with Bitcoin. Transactions are confirmed approximately ten times faster than with Bitcoin. In addition, the difficulty level of Primecoin mining is adjusted very slightly after every block.

Primecoin is not likely to catch on as a major cryptocurrency or compete toe-to-toe with Bitcoin or Ethereum, but it's an impressive work of coding that does an amazing job of showcasing a unique and useful concept.

Learn more about Primecoin at **primecoin.io**.

Namecoin (NMC)

When it comes to interesting and unique, but relatively unknown cryptocurrencies, it's difficult to beat Namecoin. It was released in April 2011 as the first project to branch off from Bitcoin. The intent of Namecoin was to allow the development of an alternative domain name service (DNS), which registers and keeps track of domain names on the Internet. Traditionally, this has been kept under centralized control by ICANN, or the Internet Corporation for Assigned Names and Numbers. The intent of Namecoin was to create a DNS which would be free from any sort of censorship and free from ICANN's control. In other words, Namecoin was developed as a means of protecting and, in some manner, *enforcing* free speech. Every domain name established by way of Namecoin ends with the *.bit* extension, which serves the same purpose as the more familiar *.com* or *.net* domains.

As cryptocurrencies, Bitcoin and Namecoin have almost no differences. For example, both will cap at 21 million individual units. Namecoin and Bitcoin are so similar that they actually share the same cryptographic techniques, allowing enterprising miners to swap between the two depending upon which is more profitable at any given moment.

Beyond the initial purpose of establishing an alternate decentralized domain name system, Namecoin can also be used as a means to set up blockchain support for things such as messaging and even voting. The system is built with versatility in mind and aims to provide as many possibilities as it can insofar as they pertain to Namecoin's particular niche.

Learn more about Namecoin at **namecoin.org**.

NEM(XEM) and Mijin

NEM is a cryptocurrency and blockchain platform, which at first was intended as a fork of NXT, but instead was built from the ground up. It offers many of the same services as NXT, but its architecture is significantly different. An associated technology, Mijin, is a private blockchain designed specifically for the banking sector.

NEM uses a new method of block verification known as proof of importance or PoI. It is designed to be even less resource-intensive than proof of stake algorithms, which NXT uses, and a lot less than proof of work algorithms, which Bitcoin uses. Like NXT, PoI can run on pretty much any machine, even a Raspberry Pi. The nature of the algorithm also encourages people to use their tokens rather than just keeping them waiting for the value to appreciate. NEM has a dedicated mobile wallet to encourage using NEM's token (designated as XEM) for everyday purchases.

NEM is designed to be more secure and much faster than Bitcoin. Developers are also working on incorporating smart contracts, such as Ethereum offers, into the NEM system. Additionally, NEM is the first major crypto platform to provide support for private blockchain development.

That's where Mijin comes in. It is a private blockchain offering faster transaction times and major improvements in efficiency. Like Ripple, Mijin represents one of the first cryptocurrency technologies to be considered by the mainstream financial industry and, moreover, suggests the possible acceptance of cryptocurrencies as a form of exchange equal to physical fiat currency.

Nem's website is **nem.io,** and information on Mijin can be found at **mijin.io**.

IOTA (MIOTA)

IOTA completely rewrites the concept of the blockchain. Whereas the typical blockchain has a linked chain of unique blocks, each storing different, but sequential information, the IOTA system depends on a *tangle* architecture. In a tangle, any given block will point to the two blocks prior to it, creating a super strong and secure data collection. This allows an infinitely scaling system of transactions. Moreover, since there are no blocks, there are no transaction costs. The last major boon that IOTA provides is the potential for transactions to occur outside of the context of the world wide web. IOTA hopes to leverage the "Internet of Things" (IoT) into the tangle.

IOTA could be a major driving force to allow Internet-enabled household appliances to communicate with one another, both to process transactions on the tangle and to make the end user's life easier. As IOTA is still in the process of being fully developed, it may be premature to delve into its details just now, but the technology shows great promise.

IOTA's website is **iota.org**.

Monero

Monero, like Dash, is intended to offer more anonymity than Bitcoin, but may in fact be more effective at it than Dash is. Originally developed as a fork of the cryptocurrency Bytecoin, it launched in April 2014 as *BitMonero*, taking the word *bit* and combining it with the Esperanto word for *coin*, "monero". Bytecoin, which still exists as a minor player in the crypto world, was a privacy-focused fork of Bitcoin.

Monero comes chock full of numerous privacy features. First, ring signatures are used to hide the wallet address of the person sending Monero, which means that the sending wallet cannot be tracked. Next, a new technology, RingCT or Ring Confidential Transactions, will hide specific information pertaining to the transaction, such as the amount transferred. Lastly, the receiving address is also obfuscated. These privacy features have helped Monero to jump into the top 10 cryptocurrencies by market capitalization, with a $1.7 billion market cap.

Find out more about Monero at **getmonero.org**.

Stratis (STRAT)

Stratis has only just recently debuted, but it has already reached a market capitalization of half a billion dollars. That's quite impressive for a newcomer to the cryptocurrency world. Stratis has become popular for two reasons. First, the Stratis development platform offers allows decentralized applications to be created within the platform, meaning that coders have a whole new set of tools to experiment with blockchains and cryptocurrencies. Perhaps more impressive, Stratis gives private organizations the ability to establish their own blockchains, which can then integrate with these new applications as well as the main Stratis blockchain. This offers an easy entry into the world of blockchains to anyone interested in experimenting with it.

Learn more about Stratis at **stratisplatform.com**.

Counterparty (XCP)

Counterparty isn't a cryptocurrency in and of itself. It does have a token, XCP, that can be bought, sold, or traded, but this capability is actually a byproduct of Counterparty's true purpose. Counterparty is a Bitcoin-based platform where new coins and other assets can be created on top of the Bitcoin blockchain. They are not Bitcoins themselves, but they use the same transaction process. They can also be used in conjunction with standard Bitcoin addresses, which simplifies accounting for the end users. Despite these shared resources, one's Counterparty and Bitcoin wallet balances exist independently of one another.

At the height of its popularity there were dozens, if not hundreds, of Counteryparty-based tokens. There were tokens representing video game assets, IOU's for digital and physical goods, voting rights in businesses and organizations, access to members-only portions of websites, and so on.

The predecessor to STORJ, SCJX, which was discussed earlier, was originally built on the Counterparty platform. A lesser known example of a Counterparty-created currency is LTBcoin, which was introduced by the hosts of the popular Bitcoin podcast, Let's Talk Bitcoin. They use the currency as a means of thanking those who help them in one way or another with the podcast. Using LTBcoin gives the user a substantial discount for podcast services as well as at various online stores that LTB has partnered with. It can also be used for tipping. It's a good example of a cryptocurrency intended only for a specific set of users.

Counterparty's official website is **counterparty.io**.

Zcoin (XZC)

Zcoin is a new cryptocurrency with a history that only stretches back to September of 2016. Like many others, Zcoin is an attempt to bring enhanced privacy to the cryptocurrency sphere. It is an implementation of the Zerocoin protocol created by professor Matthew Green of Johns Hopkins university in 2014. Zerocoin technology was originally intended to be added in Bitcoin, but was instead implemented as a separate coin, Zcoin, by Poramin Insom in 2016.

Unlike other attempts at anonymity which rely on obscuring transactions by mixing them with other transactions, units of the Zcoin currency are created on demand with no previous transaction history, and then destroyed after being used. Zcoin's operation requires lots of complex encryption, but the end result is a cryptocurrency that cannot be traced. Its objective may be shared by many other currencies in this book, but its approach is novel. Zcoin is worth keeping an eye on.

Zcoin's website is **zcoin.io**.

Ark (ARK)

ARK is a self-described "sandbox of blockchains" that seeks to be a network and platform upon which other cryptocurrencies are built. Ark uses smartbridges to connect to other blockchain-based currencies like Bitcoin and Ethereum, giving users the ability to transfer value among altcoins with a simple transaction. It has a number of as-yet undeveloped features on the development roadmap, including a dropbox-like file system, smart card integration, and enhanced privacy via the use of bridges to other blockchains. More importantly, the Ark team comprises a number of well-known crypto-developers devoted to bringing the features to life. While Ark's eventual feature set seems mostly targeted toward developers, Ark's intent is to become a very consumer-friendly end-user currency. Ark wants to attract developers with features and ease of development on their platform. Developers will, in turn, create blockchains with features that end users actually want (such as enhanced privacy). These blockchains will all be interconnected by Ark via the smartbridges.

Ark was launched in March of 2017. More information is available on their website at **ark.io**.

Chapter 9: Investing

It is impossible to discuss cryptocurrency without someone bringing up the topic of investing. The questions are universal: Should I invest? How much? Is now a good time, or should I wait? Have I missed the boat on investing altogether? Which currencies are worth buying? Where and how do I buy them?

Normally I sidestep these questions by pointing out that an introductory text is not the proper place to seek investment guidance. I usually follow that up with my standard advice that: 1) You shouldn't invest in things you do not understand, and 2) You shouldn't invest money in cryptocurrency that you can't afford to lose.

Most people aren't satisfied with that advice. People are making hundreds, thousands, and millions of dollars trading cryptocurrency, so it's only natural to be curious on the topic, even if you don't actually plan on investing at all. So, to the crypto-curious who what to know what I think, I will offer my opinion here.

But first, a disclaimer:

Disclaimer: I am not a financial or investment adviser. This chapter is general advice only. It has been prepared without taking into account your objectives, financial situation or needs. Before acting on this advice you should consider its appropriateness in regard to your own objectives, financial situation and needs.

Now that that's out of the way, let's talk.

The currencies listed in this book were chosen because I either found them interesting, innovative or thought they had historical significance. "Interesting" and "innovative" do not necessarily equate to having a future of ten- or hundred-fold increases in value. "Historical significance" could easily mean that a particular currency's race has already been run. In short: you shouldn't take an altcoin's presence in this (or any) book as a recommendation to buy.

However, of the coins discussed here, there are definitely some that I would recommend to an investor who's financial objectives and risk tolerances were similar to mine. If I were given a sum of money and told to buy some of the currencies in this book, here are the ones I would absolutely buy:

Bitcoin: Bitcoin is an elder statesman; a blue-chip stock of cryptocurrency. I think there is still a lot of upward potential and consider any price less than $10,000 a bargain. This is only a 2X to 3X increase in value from its current levels, so, while there is money to be made, it probably won't be the life-changing windfall that people want it to be.

Ethereum: The DAO debacle, the associated hard-fork, and my own skepticism kept me out of Ethereum until recently. That was a mistake. Once I dug deeper and saw the real capabilities of this platform, I realized that, early stumbles aside, it is better than Bitcoin with even more upside potential.

These two currencies would make up the bulk of my portfolio. These are my "Buy and Forget" investments. I expect both of these coins to be around and trending upward for a very long time. I have confidence enough to ignore short term pull-backs or fluctuations in value, assuming they weren't caused by some change in the fundamentals of the currency. If China decides they want to ban Bitcoin again and the price tanks, I'd use that as a chance to acquire some cheap bitcoin. That is the smart move. However, if the Bitcoin developers decide to remove the 21 million BTC cap on the number of coins, I'd jump ship, as this fundamentally changes what makes Bitcoin valuable.

Once I had taken an appropriate position in Bitcoin and Ethereum, I would diversify into one or more of the privacy-focused altcoins, such as Zcoin, Zcash, or Monero. Privacy has always been a cornerstone of cryptocurrency, and I've seen it become even more of a buzzword lately. Notice that I didn't include DASH here. I don't think DASH is a bad altcoin, but its baggage is holding it back. I'd rather back one of the newcomers. Right now, I'm rather fond of Zcoin. In the end, however, I think only a few of the privacy-focused coins will be successful. They may all continue to exist and have value, but I don't believe there is room for more than one "mainstream privacy coin". I don't know which altcoin that will be, so this is not a "buy and forget" type of investment. This is more of a "buy low and hold while watching for signals" investment. This effort, while minimal, may be more than most people are willing to undertake. That's understandable. Not everyone wants to be a trader, and not everyone wants to spend an hour reading about cryptocurrency every day. Those people should stick with Bitcoin and Ethereum.

Finally, there are several coins that I might not buy right now, but I would definitely want to learn some more about. They might be worth taking a position in… or they might not. But they are worth looking at. These coins are IOTA and ARK. Each of these has ambitions to bring needed features to areas undeserved or ignored by cryptocurrency. They are not alone in these ambitions… but they have shown more marketing and/or development effort than most of their competitors.

You can purchase most of the currencies in this book at Bittrex (**https://bittrex.com**). Exchanges are usually made between Bitcoin or Ethereum and the currency in question. I do not use Bittrex to purchase Bitcoin itself; instead, I use Coinbase (**www.coinbase.com**). I am not affiliated with either of these companies except as a customer. My willingness to mention them here is based on my personal experience, not on any investigation or examination performed by me or anyone else. You should NEVER leave cryptocurrency on an exchange after making a purchase. Always... ALWAYS... transfer your currency to a wallet that you control. Exchanges like Bittrex and Coinbase are for buying cyprotocurrency, not storing or using cryptocurrency. **Bitcoin's history** is full of examples of what happens when people ignore this advice. Don't be an example, and don't say you weren't warned.

This concludes the investing chapter of a book that probably shouldn't have an investing chapter. Go back and read the warnings and disclaimers that you skipped over on your way here. People who are brand new to cryptocurrency... I.e., the target audience of this book... shouldn't be putting their money into it. Don't invest in anything you don't understand. Don't invest money in digital currencies that you can't afford to lose. If you are going to invest in cryptocurrencies, make sure that you carefully research the topic and the specific assets you wish to buy. Cryptocurrency markets are very volatile, and there are few guarantees that a particular asset will survive more than a few years after its launch. Wise investments, however, can be quite profitable, as recent history has proven.

Further Research

Thank you for reading *Cryptocurrency: A Primer*.

This book was intended to provide a basic level of education on cryptocurrency. It is not an exhaustive exploration of all the available cryptocurrencies, a technical treatise on how blockchains work, or a guide to using them securely. This book's target audience is new users, and most new users don't need that level of detail at the start. However, if you've gotten this far you've graduated from the level of mere "crypto-curiosity," and are now ready to learn some of those details.

So where do you go from here?

I've included links to the official websites of each of the currencies I've discussed. Some of those pages, especially those of the lesser-known altcoins, are filled with marketing hype or technical jargon that you might not be ready for. Most, however, have videos that have simple explanations of the altcoin's features. If you're after technical information, search the websites for links to whitepapers. Most cryptocurrencies have one, and reading it is a bare minimum for anyone wanting to invest.

If you want more detailed but still newbie-friendly information on Bitcoin, I suggest my collection, **Using Bitcoin,** which combines three entry-level books that cover everything from mining to setting up a wallet. Each of the books in the collection is also available separately. Visit my Amazon Author page at **bit.ly/EricMorse** for my complete catalog. I will be publishing a book on Ethereum later this year.

Youtube can be a goldmine of information on all aspects of cryptographies. Unfortunately, you'll need to wade through a lot of misinformation, hype, and sales pitches to find anything useful. Rather than overwhelming you with an exhaustive list of videos and channels, I'm only going to recommend two people. The first is Andreas Antonopolos. You can find his channel at **https://www.youtube.com/user/aantonop**. Andreas has been speaking to end users, developers, bankers, and politicians for years about cryptocurrency. He does an excellent job of tailoring his talks to the level of his audience, and he is one of the smartest men in crypto. Any video with this name and face on it is worth watching. My second recommendation is a relatively new channel called DataDash run by Nicholas Merten. The channel's URL is rather unwieldy, so I've used a shortener to make it easier: **http://bit.ly/data-dash**. Nicholas focuses on the investing side of cryptocurrency. He has videos examining and introducing new altcoins, and also has very detailed lessons on trend analysis and market signals. I don't agree with all of his recommendations, but I will say without reservation that if you want to be a cryptocurrency investor, DataDash is where you should start. Between Andreas and Nicholas, you have access to enough information to make you an expert.

Thanks again for reading. May your cryptocurrency journey be interesting and profitable.

www.ingramcontent.com/pod-product-compliance
Lightning Source LLC
Chambersburg PA
CBHW070902070326
40690CB00009B/1964